# DIASPORA

Volume L

*a Las Piñas fictionary*

IVY ALVAREZ

Paloma Press, 2019

Copyright © 2019 by Ivy Alvarez

ALL RIGHTS RESERVED.

No part of this book may be reproduced or transmitted in any form or by any means, electronic or mechanical, including photocopying, recording, or by any information storage and retrieval system, without the proper written permission of the copyright owner unless such copying is expressly permitted by federal copyright law. With the exception of nonprofit transmission in Braille, Paloma Press is not authorized to grant permission for further uses of copyrighted selections reprinted in this book without the permission of their owners. Permission must be obtained from the individual copyright owners as identified herein.

ISBN 978-1-7323025-5-6

Cover & Interior Design by C. Sophia Ibardaloza

Vintage images have been digitally rendered under the Fair Use permit. Images on pages 18, 44, & 46 are from the author's private collection.

ALSO FROM PALOMA PRESS:

*Blue* by Wesley St. Jo & Remé Grefalda
*Manhattan: An Archaeology* by Eileen R. Tabios
*Anne with an E & Me* by Wesley St. Jo
*Humors* by Joel Chace
*My Beauty is an Occupiable Space* by Anne Gorrick & John Bloomberg-Rissman
*peminology* by Melinda Luisa de Jesús
*Close Apart* by Robert Cowan
*One, Two, Three: Selected Hay(na)ku Poems* by Eileen R. Tabios, trans. into Spanish by Rebeka Lembo (Bilingual Edition)
*HAY(NA)KU 15*, an anthology edited by Eileen R. Tabios
*HUMANITY*, an anthology edited by Eileen R. Tabios
*The Great American Novel* by Eileen R. Tabios
*The Good Mother of Marseille* by Christopher X. Shade

PALOMA PRESS
San Mateo & Morgan Hill, California
Publishing Poetry+Prose since 2016
www.palomapress.net

# CONTENTS

| | |
|---|---|
| Labanán ng mga pusò | 5 |
| Labás-masok | 7 |
| Labí ng aso | 9 |
| Labí ng hukay | 11 |
| Lagót ang pisì | 13 |
| Lakad-susô | 15 |
| Lakí sa lansangan | 17 |
| Lakí sa nunò | 19 |
| Lálabasán | 21 |
| Lamáng-kati | 23 |
| Landás na matiník | 25 |
| Langaw at gatas | 27 |
| Langís-langisán | 29 |
| Langit at lupà | 31 |
| Langit ng buhay | 33 |
| Lantáng bulaklák | 35 |
| Lawít ang pusod | 37 |
| Layláy ang balikat | 39 |
| Lígaw-intsík | 41 |
| Lígaw-tingín | 43 |
| Ligong-pato | 45 |
| Liping-mahál | 47 |
| Lumálakí ang ulo | 49 |
| Lumang tugtugin | 51 |
| Lumílipád ang isip | 53 |
| Lumílipád pa sa alapaap | 55 |
| Lumuluhà ng bató | 57 |
| Acknowledgements | 59 |
| About the Author | 61 |

# Labanán ng mga pusò

Cock-fighting rooster-comb reds, blood-filled retreating,
advance that's tidal, conceding promises like plates,
flocked wallpaper, discard aplenty and I confess,
dance around the subject: I don't want to hear your bleating.
My hand, a volume turned up high, a cleft and these crates
of memory, put out, kerbside. Balcony stretch, a right mess,
by heaven's mercy, address how there's naught to be found, only
love, or remnants thereof, or rumours thereof, or not.
An abundance of crockery, cutlery, paired up or lonely,
unthrown, sometimes maculate. The cat cares not a jot.
Can we forgive? Why not? Exceptions in plenitude.
Unknown peace, unshown keys to harmony. Yes?
Yes. We once cup and saucer. Now paper plate disposable. Not rude,
just less notice, less words said, less eyes met, less and less.

*Filipino idiom meaning avoiding conversation between two lovers (literally, conflict of the hearts)*

## Labás-masok

Frigid air fogs my skin. I stand in front of this often,
obeisant. Perhaps something new this time
since the last time I looked.

I want to be full. Either there's plenty
or there's nothing. Perhaps it is the door
opening and closing that soothes me.

*Filipino idiom meaning more or less (literally, going in and out)*

## Labí ng aso

we dreamt the same thing, love
didn't we? we must have done
we ran away, but only I came back
father killed my dog and ate it
placed for me on a white plate
its black salty lips

*Filipino idiom meaning lady who eloped with a man and then returned to her parents (literally, leftover of the dog)*

## Labí ng hukay

candles lit like tears
a forest of legs                murmuring
I am shepherded            away from the white box
the paint pearly               that is all I can see

*Filipino idiom meaning grave (literally, lip of dug soil)*

# Lagót ang pisì

to say it aloud invites superstition

the coins might be missing but the feeling wasn't

there was bounty under my feet

I often ate the sky and the sea

so don't say it

I only felt hunger scrape my belly in an affluent country

through no fault of my own

*Filipino idiom meaning penniless (literally, thread is cut)*

# Lakad-susô

strolling          without destination
afternoon burnt    by midday sun
post-siesta        pre-dinner
dragging one's sandals on the ground
scratching along

deny haste         amble-paced on Las Ramblas
or the avenue      or the promenade
or the boulevard

we have time       to draw out time
there'll be another tomorrow     tomorrow
for us             mud-footed
                   and slow

*Filipino idiom meaning slowfoot (literally, snail pace)*

## Lakí sa lansangan

what would you know about the street
the vulcanology of the early
                        how it narrates
                        a childhood
the fireworks        the welding
before anyone ever added anything
ingredients for a clear brown broth
complicated in the way a potato has eyes
everyone looks and a car doesn't see
its tyre ran over my toe my bicycle wheel
from then on I learned not to say
my father's name        there's an etiquette
to saying it

*Filipino idiom meaning bad-mannered (literally, grew up in the street)*

# Lakí sa nunò

a parallel world easing
everything cutting
into the roundedness of snow
forgives ugliness
bestows wonder and shine
places amnesias on children's tongues
melting like sacrament
swallow like blood
the rightness of rock
begetting smaller stones
the accrual of grit
as it goes

*Filipino idiom meaning pampered (literally, grew up with grandparents)*

# Lálabasán

to be told
I am an adjective
does not make me
that adjective
no matter how complimentary
or inflationary the adjective

beneath the skin
fluid will expel
the splinter out
               protect the body

beauty is a genius
of aesthetics
intelligence a splinter
some foreign matter

a movement
from one state
to another

*Filipino idiom meaning has ability or intelligence (literally, something will come out)*

## Lamáng-kati

Asseveration is natural to me.
A machete, too — blackness
bonding to metal like rust.
I've seen blood on dirt.
It doesn't hurt.

The first time I heard the words
dog's breakfast, it made sense to me.
Things can get so messy
only a dog would eat it up.

The meat market's wash and slurry,
my feet brown with storm water,
the aisles lined with heads, limbs:
a wedding I never knew.

Let's not make a hash of love —
that's not how it ends,
what the shore looks like after hard rain,
the sea disgorging its contents.

*Filipino idiom meaning meat of butchered animals (literally, contents of low tide)*

## Landás na matiník

out and inside the sting
mouth floods burst juice
membranous iron undercurrent
of blood don't worry explain it to me
when you're five everything is more itself
at the time the flavour of warnings
every needle full of poison
prickles nestled winkled out
from its hiding place
worth eating well

*Filipino idiom meaning difficulties (literally, thorny path)*

## Langaw at gatas

Who could understand the attraction between milk and a fly? He had smelled the cream within my skin, he said. And I loved the danger in him. His dirt. His grime. I can't be pure all the time. He made me spill myself again and again. He hovered above me, dirty, strange, grit falling all around us. He stopped me being blank. And I, I drowned him, drowned him. He swam in my shimmer as, eventually, the afternoon grew dimmer and dimmer.

*Filipino idiom that applies to a couple, where the man is ugly and the woman is beautiful (literally, fly and milk)*

## Langís-langisán

As a hand's cupful of oil drizzle-drops on top of skin, he watches it slide. She feels it slip to her sides, while he tries to win her over, combining his hands and the right amount of pressure to release each deep knot tied up inside her. He is warming her up to the idea of him being there, beside her, with his palms on her, while she considers the *if*s, and *should she*s. Enumerates the consequences. There is continuance, resistance, and then, perhaps, a letting go. Surrender to the oil, its flow, how it parts flesh, lulls nerves to thrum in one direction, relax, say yes.

*Filipino idiom meaning to win favour (literally, oil up)*

## Langit at lupà

When they loved, these lovers, the earth rose to meet them. An undulating hill. A split in the dirt. Deep and ravenous, warm like old lava, with all its exhalations. Penetration was a foot in the mud, with just enough liquid to suck, reluctant to release flesh, to love and lave, a flat tongue on every fold of skin.

When they argued, the world turned celestial, colloidal, cold with distant song, and stars. Not a lullaby you'd want to hear. Not to sleep, but to leach the heat from bones, sting mouths fleetly shut. Hard to imagine being warm again from so much interplanetary dust.

So they're left to wonder, wander, and covet the fall, fast, at last, to earth.

*Filipino idiom meaning opposites (literally, heaven and earth)*

# Langit ng buhay

There's a hole where the nail used to be and she can see through it, straight to heaven. Oh, she's sure he's up there, somewhere, waiting for her. She peers out the hole oh the whole time we've been talking you know, peering for the epiphany only we know and have been holding onto. If only we had the guts to tell her there's no such thing: she can't make *a heaven of life*! And if it's not a gun, it's a knife, or a lie, or the phone, or a hotel room, or a stone with a key inside it. Or he might have heaven up there with him. Or she might be his wife. Better she keep looking, press her ear eye nose throat spine elbows spleen toes through the hole and ask if she fits and keep waiting for it and we can tell her stories to pass the time.

*Filipino idiom meaning complete happiness (literally, heaven of life)*

## Lantáng bulaklák

Once picked, can you blame her? She's not the same. Yes, a shame. Not like the same thing happens to men. Once *they're* picked, they can be picked and picked again, with no consequence, no value lost or innocence gained or, at least, only less. Not enough to count. For them, each use helps to burnish what needs burnishing or, if fragile, that which requires strengthening. She, on the other hand, must contend with transparent lies, sly eyes suggesting intricate indelicacies of the wild kind. A wilted flower waits, is denied admission, is no use without bloom for butterfly or bee, for transmission of fruit and progeny. A beauty tarnished begets nothing, is less than useless. So she stays furled, closed up, tight-lipped as a bud, and furious. And who could blame her?

*Filipino idiom meaning disgraced woman (literally, withered flower)*

# Lawít ang pusod

Am I being naïve? Corkscrew tip knot nipples out, and I don't mind if people think I'm strong, you're beautiful. When your belly pouts and you want more, I respect that; the ways in which you hunger. There's no mismatch here. It meets my expectations cutaneously, with no complaint from me. When I drink from you, I taste watermelon juice. A generous gift, really. You guard everything carefully. Art. Words. Your every single possession. Even me. I like it when I can peep out occasionally, standing on the cliff by the cave of your belly button.

*Filipino idiom meaning selfish, stingy (literally, protruding navel)*

# Layláy ang balikat

When you placed the magnolia on each riser, careful not to press petals to the hue of a bruise, my skin skewed instead, knowing that ahead, at the top of the stair, revelations lay like gifts unwrapped. I've never heard of you, Mr Strong. Have you heard of me? I am Beauty. A scent coalesces at our feet. The climb feels incomplete until I say that's it. I can't afford to have your life in mine. Your shoulders droop minutely, admits my villainy. Yet we gaze to disperse each flower's perfume until every atom leaves the room and us alone.

*Filipino idiom meaning disappointed look (literally, drooping shoulders)*

## Lígaw-intsík

Maybe we can be together. Maybe I can say the words. What
can I whisper? My shoes brace against the metal gate. I am a key now

and somehow I slip in. It's not magic. Once I lift the latch,
I am inside your kitchen, up the stairs, hitching my lungs

to silent walls, the windows. The rails. Did you never wonder
how I arrived at your bed? Or did you merely accept, take

in your hands the gift of these limbs, the scent on my neck,
the throb beneath my ribs, something trying to leap out.

*Filipino idiom meaning giving gifts when courting (literally, Chinese courting)*

# Lígaw-tingín

We conduct these games covertly, an exchange of invisible coinage, a currency still unstated, the hunger in our looks unsated, so we keep carving each feature and pore, and eyelash, and more, into a certain fold in the brain. My grey matter is indelibly stained with you, a drop of dye in a glass of water, tinting everything. Every sense amplified to the level of prey, skittish, almost British, endangered, barely keeping the heart at bay from one's throat. We stay. We try and pay attention to what our eyes say, our tongues withhold.

*Filipino idiom meaning bashful courting with the eyes only (literally, courting look)*

# Ligong-pato

Let's wade into shallow water; the tea-brown creek wends to the beach. Feel how warmth covers unfamiliar skin. This is the beginning of becoming archetypal. A clinical smell overwhelms the air. Perhaps I am antiseptic, impulsive, incorruptible. Unbaptisable. You are preserved in amber water, darkening by the hour, turning into night.

*Filipino idiom meaning taking a bath without wetting the head (literally, duck bath)*

# Liping-Mahál

*Can clan clangour.* Who knows
the danger behind each cell.
How he divides, multiplies,

this rogue mischief
-maker, who'll tell
and tell a well

-placed lie, at the right
time. All the matriarchs
are on their guard.

They know what he's here for:
sow discord, lead daughters
to greater hells.

There's much expense
to be paid. A royal fuck-up
of events

could render expectations
to frowns. This high life
is costly

and looks like
they are going
down.

*Filipino idiom meaning from royal blood (literally, costly clan)*

# Lumálakí ang ulo

To grow bigger is what it means to be a man. A small boy becomes a big man, with a big head, whether or not he deserves it. A little girl becomes a small woman, the smallest possible *she* she can be. That is the ideal. Squeezed to her thinnest self. Corseted and bound, sucked, spat out by holes in heads, she cannot recognise herself. Her head is huge, the only thing she cannot shrink. Even then she is told: You must not think.

*Filipino idiom meaning arrogant (literally, growing head)*

# Lumang tugtugin

What are these seconds you bring and sing? Can't even remember when last I sinned. This morning? I'm full of questions. Split my belly and you'll find 'em, stem to stern. Around the kernel, a corner of truth, sharp as tax. When humidity burns, it's time to get out, time to subtract myself from danger's path, steam-rollering like a curling iron set too hot on my neck, your neck, our all-too-tender necks.

*Filipino idiom meaning old news (literally, old music)*

# Lumílipád ang isip

cicada glass, green-veined wings
    threads of mould, like tree roots,
feathers, papillae on my mouth
    taste buds dying, still you creak away
in the leaves, a fresh green body
    patinating verdigris, old chicken feet
simmering in broth, so salty
    I can taste nothing else

*Filipino idiom meaning straying from the topic (literally, flying mind)*

## Lumílipád pa sa alapaap

in deep water, fish are music
blowing bubbles at the sky
wide flat discs of waterlily leaves
a floating stage
for dragonflies and the like
the fish are sized
from my elbow to my wrist
eyes dark coins
(eternally open)
a muscle moves underwater
for the notes it creates
every fin conducting dreamily
aswim in clouds of silt
roiling in a chase for food
flex and bend
the clouds unburden
a timpani on the umbrella
percussing down the lily pad's stem
the waiting fish listens
looks up to see circles
rippling and rippling

*Filipino idiom meaning daydreaming (literally, still flying in the clouds)*

## Lumuluhà ng bato

the stone is female, of course

                                               a stone fits in your hand
                  a rock in your arms
                            the women fling wet clothes
                            as if to crush
             their enemies, their lives
force out water, too much liquid
                in the fabric
                              how else can it dry
pound the drowning weight
                         heavy as bodies
                         waterlogged
               the smack of the paddle
and the water gushes out
                falling down

                                *smack* smack *smack*

drops describe an arc
                and the women gather the beaten up
in their arms
                              place them in baskets
                to rest on their hips
                        balance on crowns
to thread their way between treacherous rocks

                            hang them home


*Filipino idiom meaning to suffer much (literally, the stone is crying)*

# ACKNOWLEDGEMENTS

Deepest gratitude to the editors of the following publications: *Flash Frontier* (New Zealand), *Foundry Journal*, *The Good Journal* (UK), *Phantom Billstickers Café Reader* (New Zealand), *PUÑETA: Political Pilipinx Poetry* (Moria Books, 2017), *Red Room Company* (Australia), and *Verity La* (Australia).

In 2016, "Langit ng buhay" received honourable mentions from *Blueshift Journal*, which added the poem to its Editor's List (Brutal Nation edition), and from *Glass: A Poetry Journal*, which included it in its Recommended Reading List. The poem also features in *Bonsai: Best Small Stories from Aotearoa New Zealand* (Canterbury University Press, 2018).

# ABOUT THE AUTHOR

**Ivy Alvarez** is a Fellow of MacDowell Colony (US), and Hawthornden (UK). Her work is widely published and anthologised, including two appearances in the *Best Australian Poems* series.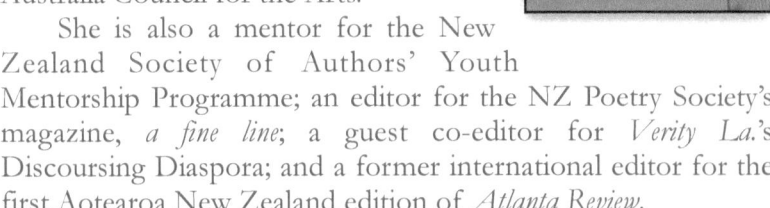

With poems translated into Russian, Spanish, Japanese, and Korean, she is a three-time Pushcart Prize nominee, and a recipient of grants from Creative New Zealand, Literature Wales, and the Australia Council for the Arts.

She is also a mentor for the New Zealand Society of Authors' Youth Mentorship Programme; an editor for the NZ Poetry Society's magazine, *a fine line*; a guest co-editor for *Verity La*.'s Discoursing Diaspora; and a former international editor for the first Aotearoa New Zealand edition of *Atlanta Review*.

Born in the Philippines and raised in Australia, Ivy Alvarez lived in Scotland, Ireland and Wales, before moving to Auckland, New Zealand in 2014.

## Books
*The Everyday English Dictionary* (London: Paekakariki Press, 2016)
*Disturbance* (Wales, UK: Seren Books, 2013)
*Mortal* (Washington, DC: Red Morning Press, 2006)

## Ephemera
*Hollywood Starlet* (Chicago: dancing girl press, 2015)
*('fi:meil) † defaced* (Australia: SOd Press, 2015)
*One Dozen Poison Hay(na)ku* (Washington, DC: Big Game Books, 2007)
*what's wrong* (Cardiff: The Private Press, 2005)
*catalogue: life as tableware* (Cardiff: The Private Press, 2004)
*Food for Humans* (Melbourne: Slow Joe Crow Press, 2002)

Established in 2016, **PALOMA PRESS** is a San Francisco Bay Area-based independent literary press publishing poetry, prose, and limited edition books. Titles include *BLUE* by Wesley St. Jo & Remé Grefalda (officially launched at The Library of Congress in September 2017), and *MANHATTAN: An Archaeology* by Eileen R. Tabios (which debuted at the 4th Filipino American International Book Festival at the San Francisco Public Library).

Paloma Press believes in the power of the literary arts, how it can create empathy, bridge divides, change the world. To this end, Paloma has released fundraising chapbooks such as *MARAWI*, in support of relief efforts in the Southern Philippines; and *AFTER IRMA AFTER HARVEY*, in support of hurricane-displaced animals in Texas, Florida and Puerto Rico. As part of the San Francisco Litquake Festival, Paloma proudly curated the wildly successful literary reading, "THREE SHEETS TO THE WIND," and raised money for the Napa Valley Community Disaster Relief Fund. In 2018, the fundraising anthology, *HUMANITY*, was released in support of UNICEF's Emergency Relief campaigns on the borders of the United States and in Syria.

www.ingramcontent.com/pod-product-compliance
Lightning Source LLC
Chambersburg PA
CBHW060506080526
44584CB00015B/1574